A Memoir of a Year with a Crow

Amy Leput Strahl

Blackie is a memoir. Some names are used with permission or changed, characters, places, and incidents are the account of the author.

Author photo by www.ericadanilephotography.com/

Published in the United States
by White Bird Publications, LLC, Austin, Texas
www.whitebirdpublications.com

Paperback ISBN 978-1-63363-523-4
eBook ISBN 978-1-63363-524-1
Library of Congress Control Number: 2021939968

PRINTED IN THE UNITED STATES OF AMERICA

Dedication

I dedicate this book to my husband, Dr. Robert C. Strahl, my anchor, strength, guiding light, and touchstone.

"Considering all these different folks, I could find only two things that they all seem to share in common—open minds that can see beyond popular stereotypes, and hearts warm enough to love friends of another species."

—Michael Westerfield, *The Language of Crows*

Table of Contents

Preface

People I meet are always surprised when they learn of my affection for crows. Like so many other folks, their view of crows is based on occasionally witnessing crows eating carrion on the roadside or plucking a baby bird out of a nest. It does not help that a flock of crows is called a "Murder." Literature has often depicted crows as being bearers of bad omens, and even Halloween portrays them as scary.

I, on the other hand, marvel at them. It is because of this diversity in attitudes that I decided to write this book. I envision the audience as children. I hope it causes children to want to learn about crows, to be curious about them, and to come to realize how truly smart and joyful they are.

I am no ornithologist. My knowledge of crows comes from reading non-fiction books about them. However, the greatest teacher I had was a crow our family, rehabbed when I was a child. Those lessons are the ones about which I write.

Over sixty years ago, my brother and I, at ages nine and six respectively, shared a year with a crow. We often refer to him as the "pet of a lifetime." Thanks to him, Blackie, and our Dad, my brother and I learned about the delicacy and viciousness of Mother Nature.

I am not an advocate of people robbing nests in order to have a pet crow. My father taught me to not interfere with Mother Nature. "Hypocrite" you say, since I referred to Blackie as a pet. When Blackie was part of our lives more than sixty years ago, there were no wildlife rehabbers. I like to think of my father as a rehabber pioneer. Proof of this will unfold throughout the book.

People may ask, is your entire book true? I ask that you keep in mind that the stories are a collection of what my brother and I jointly remember when we were youngsters. If I had to take a guess, I would say 95% of it is absolute truth. An occasional name or statement was added here and there to make it a more interesting narrative or to teach a lesson about crows.

Farmers may view crows as pests; however, I do not know of another occupation more centered around Mother Nature than farmers. As long as farmers follow local laws in how they deal with crows, I have no conflict with them.

If you are a child, I encourage you to go to a quiet space, preferably outdoors, and enjoy this book about a gift of nature as seen through the eyes of another child. Then, go and bestow your knowledge about crows to others.

Amy Leput Strahl

BLACKIE:

A Memoir of a Year with a Crow

White Bird
Publication, LLC

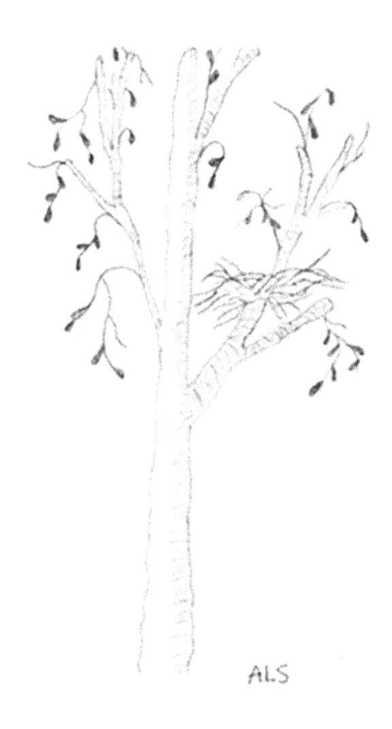

Chapter 1

The Adventure Begins

“What the heck do you expect me to do with a baby crow that has a broken wing?” asked my father, Pete. “And where did you get the thing? You better not have not robbed it from its nest.”

“Oh, heck Pete,” my father’s friend, Clyde, said. You know me better than that. It wasn’t intentional. My son and I, the one in high school, were taking down a sickly tree in the yard. Not until the tree came down did I know there was a crow's nest in it. There were three youngsters in it. Two flew off, but this little guy was on the ground squawking. My boy wanted him really bad as a pet, so we took him in."

"And?" my father asked, his voice rising.

"Things were going well, but then this ornery[1] bird thought it would be fun to land on our dog and peck his head. Dog near killed him. I was able to save the bird, but not before the dog broke the crow's wing. His wing is all bent and funny looking. See here?"

Clyde reached into the cardboard box and lifted out the young crow. Sure enough, its right wing was sticking out looking like it was ready to fly. The left wing was held firmly to his body. "I told my son he had to make a choice. He could keep the crow or the dog. Keeping them both wasn't an option."

"Let me see that thing." Dad took the baby crow from Clyde. As soon as the bird was handed over, its red mouth opened wide. Almost too wide. He started making an ear-piercing squawking sound. Louder and louder and louder. When that did not get him what he wanted, he started fluttering his one good wing.

He is so cute and funny sounding, I thought.

My brother and I looked at each other. There was a

silent agreement between the two of us. *We want to keep the crow.*

We giggled and silently hoped. After all, Dad had been known to put down[2] a sick or injured animal so it would not suffer. Many times, Dad said, "You never let an animal suffer. Never."

Walt and I hoped this bird was not suffering. "*This crow isn't doing well, but by the way he's acting, he doesn't look like he's suffering.*"

As if reading my mind, Dad ordered my brother to get some food. "Walt, go get some dog food and mix it up with warm water. Bring it here when it's good and soft."

"Shouldn't we get it some bird food?" I asked.

"Amy, this is a crow. Crows are considered to be pillagers. Do you know what that means?"

I did not say anything, but I must have had a confused look on my face.

"Pillagers," Dad said, "are animals that will eat practically anything. They will eat roadkill,[3] eggs, snails, grain, insects, snakes, corn, baby birds, crayfish, even rodents. They are not picky eaters like some little girl I know who won't eat liver put before her," my father said, winking at me.

"Birds, like this crow, are important to nature. They are like Mother Nature's garbage men. They go around and pick up dead plants and animals. They get rid of nature's waste. Think about what this world would be like if they didn't do their job. There would be dead plants and animals lying everywhere. Crows don't need special bird food. Like us, they just need to eat a variety of food. For now, you and your brother can give him dog food. When Walt comes back with the dog food, roll it into small balls, and put them into his gaping mouth one-by-one."

A devilish idea crossed my mind and I grinned. "Can I give him some of my liver next time Mom serves it?"

"No," Dad said loudly.

And that settled that.

As Walt and I squished up the dog food into little globs and took turns feeding the crow, we eavesdropped on Dad and Clyde's conversation.

"Blackie," Walt whispered. "Blackie. We're naming him Blackie."

"How did Walt know that was the exact name I was considering?" Our family tends to use adjectives[4] as pet names. We have had a Nosey, a Fuzzy, and a Peppy.

We heard bits and pieces of what Dad and Clyde were

discussing.

"He's still a young bird," Dad said. "His eyes are still blue. They haven't yet turned brown and look at his mouth. When he opens it up while the kids feed him, the inside is still bright red and his gape[5] is still pink. Even his beak is still pale. He definitely needed some more time with his parents."

"I know, Pete. That's why I brought him to you. I figured with all your experience with pigeons, you'd know how to care for a crow. How different can it be?"

Dad gave Clyde a disgusted look. "Clyde, the only thing those two birds have in common is the fact that they are both smart birds. Period. That is it."

Dad would know. He had told us stories about when he was young and raised pigeons. He even raced them. He was so well known as a pigeon racer, that when he went into the Army in 1942, he was assigned to the Pigeon Corps.

Some people scoff[6] at the idea of training pigeons for the Army, but Dad always said, "What those fools don't know is how different communication was during World War II. My birds had a 90% success rate relaying messages about troop activity. Because of my pigeons, many soldiers' lives were saved. My birds didn't rely on wires or radio signals. They relied on their smarts, senses, and relationship with me."

"All right, all right Clyde, we'll care for the bird but not before Walt and I build him a safe shelter."

And so, it happened. Clyde took the crow home, cared for him, and waited for my Dad and Walt to build an a-v-i-a-r-y. I learned that an aviary is a fancy way of saying a large bird cage. They took half-inch wire mesh and some scrap wood and built a safe home for Blackie. It had an opening through which he could go in and out.

"Aren't we going to put in a door, Dad?" Walt asked.

"No, that bird's wing will heal, and he will need to learn how to fly and forage[7] for his own food. He'll venture out when he's hungry and strong, but in the meantime, he will know he always has a safe place to stay. Kind of like a new nest."

Walt and Dad anchored the cage to an elm tree. It was up pretty high. I could not touch its entrance way, and I was pretty tall for a six-year-old girl.

"Daddy, how is Blackie going to be able to get into his cage if he can't fly? His entranceway is up too high. Did you forget?" I asked.

Just as the words came out, Walt came walking down

the hill from the garage carrying the strangest looking thing. In his hands was a long, narrow eight-foot piece of wood. About every two inches, going in the opposite direction, was an attached piece of wood going from one end to the other.

"Blackie has a set of steps!" I screamed with delight.

"It's more like a step ladder." My brother corrected me.

Walt and my Dad took some time setting the bottom of Blackie's ladder on the ground, and then they attached the top of it soundly to the entrance of the cage. When it was secured in place, I was told to get two metal bowls. One for food and one for water.

While Dad telephoned Clyde to tell him we were ready to care for the crow, Walt showed me how strong and secure the cage and its ladder were. We both smiled with excitement. It was time to get Blackie!

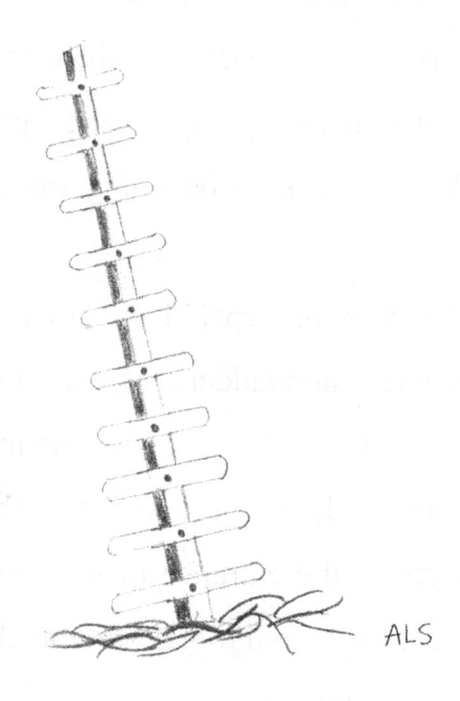

Chapter 2

Earning Trust

Clyde brought Blackie to us in a cardboard box punched full of holes. Our young crow was not happy to be confined.[8] We could hear him squawking, screaming, and giving a high-pitched caw as soon as Clyde took the box out of his car. It sounded as if Blackie was having a temper tantrum.

Dad took the box from Clyde, then the three of us followed Dad to the backyard. Clyde was impressed with the aviary Walt and Dad had made. It was large enough for Blackie to jump from one twig to another on the perches we had set up, and he could get to the food and water dishes set on the cage's bottom without trouble.

"How in the world is Daddy going to get the angry bird into its new home?" I whispered to Walt.

"He used to raise and race pigeons Amy. Dad knows how to handle birds."

And he did. Dad reached his powerful hands deep into the box. We could hear a lot of scurrying of claws and baby-sounding caws coming from within. Dad's voice got gentle. He started muttering calming words to Blackie. I do not know what the words were, but they had a soothing effect on Blackie. Once the scampering stopped, Dad brought out our bird. He held the bird's legs together and kept the bird close to his chest. Dad continued with his gentle sounds and rubbed the bird's head. Walt and I stepped closer for our turn to pet him.

After a little while, Dad said, "That's enough now. This bird has been through a lot today. Let me put him into his cage. Let him get used to his new home. If you want to watch him, do it from a distance. Sit up on the hill, but don't go near his cage. Every day you two can skootch a little closer to his aviary. When he feels comfortable, he will come out to you. For now, let me feed him. If he pecks at my hands, they can take it. He'll calm down. You two just have to be patient."

Dad was right. It only took a week. From a distance, Walt and I would watch Blackie jump from perch to perch and side to side within his cage. If his food dish was empty, he would pick it up with his beak and throw it onto the cage's floor. It was as if he was telling us he was hungry and needed more food. He ate anything that was put into his food bowl. Dog food kibbles, hard boiled eggs, nightcrawlers Walt and I found for him, wild cherries, and even dried corn.

There was one food Blackie did not like. He would not eat broccoli. Walt and I watched as he picked up a piece, threw it to the cage floor, and then took it to the entrance and dropped it outside. Walt and I put broccoli in his dish just for the entertainment value of watching Blackie get rid of it.

One day our patience was rewarded. Walt and I were sitting about ten feet from his cage when Blackie stuck his head out the entrance. He warily put one foot onto the ladder leading to his cage. It was as if he was testing its stability.[9] Then he put the other foot onto it. Step by step, he inched his way sideways down the entire length of the ladder. Walt and I sat quietly, wanting to scream with excitement but knowing better. Blackie hopped towards us. Then he inched between us. Walt and I mimicked the utterances[10] we heard our father say. He enjoyed the gentle strokes we gave him. He put his head down as if to show us the back of his head where he wanted to be rubbed. We all stayed like that for a few minutes. After a bit, Blackie hopped back to his ladder and confidently walked up the steps and back into his cage. Walt and I ran back to our house.

"We did it! We did it Mom," we screamed. "We won Blackie's trust."

Mom smiled. "Yes, you did."

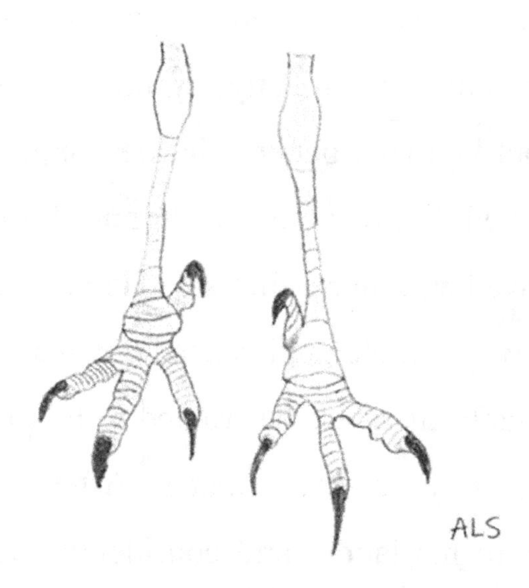

Chapter 3

Crow's Feet and Playfulness

The rest of the summer was one of learning. Blackie taught us. We, unknowingly, taught him. Blackie would venture out of his cage and flutter step behind us. From time to time he tried to use his wings, but he quickly stopped and settled back to the ground. He flapped and walked and hopped and fluttered, trying to keep up with us as we played in our backyard.

Our friends loved visiting Blackie. Walt would instruct them to put their arm real low to the ground and if Blackie liked them, he would hop onto the outstretched arm and then sidestep up their arm.

Blackie had an uncanny[11] sense of identifying good people, bad people, and fearful people. Good people were greeted with one or two caws. Those caws were not harsh. They sounded to me like they were saying, "Hi, Walt!" or "Hi, Amy!"

Bad people, like a neighbor kid, Jimmy, would be scolded. We could tell if Jimmy was venturing into our yard by the racket Blackie would make. Those caws were earsplitting. Mean even. Those grating[12] caws were accompanied with scary-looking body language.[13] Blackie would move his head up and down, fluff out his feathers so that he looked twice his size, and he would flap his wings. Not to fly. More as a warning. As mean as Jimmy was, even he was afraid of our watchdog crow.

Several times, too many to count, neighbors' dogs would come wandering into our yard. When they dared, it seemed as if Blackie recalled when Clyde's dog broke his wing.

As soon as Blackie spotted a dog enter our yard, he zoomed down his ladder, snuck up, and pulled the dog's tail. The startled dog turned around, and Blackie made a hop flap back. This would go on and on. The dog would turn his back to the crow, and Blackie would continue his torment.

As Blackie healed, his teasing of dogs increased. Soon he was able to jump onto dogs' backs. As much as a dog would try to get Blackie off, the pooch could never reach him. The dog looked like he was chasing his own tail as he spun in circles trying to get the crow off his back. Eventually, the exhausted dog would pause. That is when Blackie really tormented the dog. He would inch his way up the dog's back towards his head and peck at his noggin.[14] I am not talking gentle pecks. I am talking wanting to drill a hole in your head stabs. Those duels usually ended with the dog skedaddling out of our yard, and Blackie falling off the dog's back. This happened every single time a dog ventured into our yard. Like I said, Blackie had a sense of knowing good from bad from fearful.

That summer was filled with learning about a crow's growth and changes as it matured. We learned about crow's behaviors too. Blackie's blue eyes changed to clear brown, and the inside of his mouth changed from red to black. He grew and grew. When Blackie landed upon my arm, I could gauge[15] his size. Beak to tail tip, he was the length of my arm. When he would extend his wings and exercise his flapping, he would bop me in the face.

His tail was shaped like a fan, and come late summer, Walt and I spotted fallen feathers on the grass. Blackie was going through his first molt. About once a year, a crow's feathers will fall out one by one, and new ones replace them. New feathers are called pin feathers, and they are fragile. Dad told us not to handle Blackie too much during his molt. After his new feathers had grown in, they were so shiny that they looked silvery.

He was one patient and trusting bird with Walt and me. After his molt, Blackie allowed us to stretch and spread out his wings and inspect his flight feathers. We could ease him on his back and move his belly feathers so we could see under them. They almost looked whitish under there. Blackie was tolerant with all of our gentle, curious pokes and prodding. Walt and I thought Blackie's knees bent backwards. When Walt and I proclaimed this to Mom, she said we should look it up in the encyclopedia.

"Can you do it for us, Mom?"

She smiled, shook her head. "No," she said. "You'll find it under 'C'."

And so we did. Blackie's knees did not bend backwards. What we thought were his knees were really his ankles and heel bone. His knees were hidden from view and were much farther up his leg under his feathers almost near his ribs.

We also learned that crows have built in eye goggles. Crows do not just have two eyelids, top and bottom, like we do. Crows have a third eyelid that moves horizontally from one corner of the eye to the other. We learned to pay close attention when Blackie blinked his eyes. That was the only time we could see it. It was as fast as a windshield wiper. It is funny looking. It is pale bluish in color and almost see-through. Dad taught us that crows can see through it. It is there to protect their eyes and keep them moist.

We also learned that crows love to take baths. Walt and I had a huge aluminum saucer-shaped sled that was one of our favorites for sledding. We set it out within Blackie's view. We filled it up with fresh water every day. About three times a week Blackie walked down his ladder and ventured to his bathtub. He hopped onto its edge and took several sips of the clean water. He then lifted his head as he swallowed the cool, fresh water. That crow of ours even made sipping water a joyful experience. He would then wade into his tub. He would crouch down low into it, then dip his head into the water and flap his wings as if he were slapping the water. He would shake himself quickly causing droplets of water to fly every which way. His baths lasted several minutes, then he would hop back onto edge of the sled and shake again until he was nearly dry. While waiting to dry, he poked at the base of his tail and then ruffled each feather. It was as if he were putting something on each feather and then setting it back to its proper place.

When we told Mom about this behavior, she taught us it was called "preening" and directed us to look under "P" in the encyclopedia. Sure enough, preening is when birds spread oil, found near their tails, all over their feathers to make them water resistant and make sure their feathers are positioned properly.

Watching Blackie taking a bath was fun and educational. I guess in a way, he should also get credit for teaching Walt and me how to use an encyclopedia.

Chapter 4

Black Things

As September approached, Mom and Dad made our bedtime earlier and earlier. Their thinking was they wanted us to get used to an earlier bedtime once our days were filled with school, lessons, and learning.

Our school, Foxcroft, sat on top of the hill from our house. It was about a half mile from our home, so we walked there and back. Up the hill in the morning and down the hill in the afternoon. Like we were taught, we walked on the left-side of the road in order to face traffic. All our neighborhood friends would walk up the hill together. The first week or so, while we were in school, Blackie just hung around our backyard doing crow things. Soon enough his curiosity must have gotten to him. He probably wondered why we were not playing with him all day as we had during the summer.

One day he followed us to school. Yep, he waddled and hopped right along with us up the street and to school. He stayed at school for a little while and then disappeared. When we got home, he would be foraging through the grass for bugs to eat and cawing. This continued on and on every day. Sometimes he would stay at school, hoping to find lunch scraps.

There was a lady whose house was along our route to school. I did not know what language she spoke, but boy, she liked to clean. Every day she washed the windows in her house. Every single day! When she spotted Blackie walking on her grass, she stuck her head and fist outside the window and yelled and shook her fist. I did not know what she was saying, but it did not sound friendly or kind. Walt and I understood a little bit of Polish from listening to all our grandparents, parents, uncles, and aunts speak it. This neighbor lady wasn't speaking Polish. Whatever language she spoke, it sounded mean.

One day she was outside waiting for us. She stood in her front yard with a hand on her hip. Again, she started yelling and sputtering. The only words I understood were "black" and "evil." As hard as I tried, I could not understand anything else she said, but when she flicked her cleaning rag at Blackie chasing him onto the street, I got her drift. Unsure what I was going to do about it, at least I understood her. Blackie's presence on her lawn was unwanted. Every day our group of friends kept taking our usual route to school, walking on the left side of the road, and every day she continued to yell at Blackie while we ignored her.

One morning, on our way to school, Blackie spotted something in the lady's yard that was irresistible[16] to him. It was an ant mound. He walked over to it and squatted down low. He began flapping his wings. Ants and tiny pearls of dirt were tossed everywhere. Our gang of friends walked up to Blackie to get a closer look. He was covered in ants. Hundreds of black ants were crawling all over him, and he was enjoying it! He rolled onto his side and flicked again. He did this over and over again. At times, he would poke his beak into the ant hill's opening which really angered the ants. I swear Blackie was smiling. Each time he flapped his wings, the mess would be spread farther, even reaching onto the lady's sidewalk.

How could a creature have ants running all over its body and enjoy it? As Walt and I bent lower to inspect Blackie, the lady came bursting out her screen door. She looked different this time. Not only was she angry, she was menacing.[17] Again, we heard her shout "evil" and "black." This time we were afraid she might hurt Blackie, not just shush him, so we nudged our crow until he hopped to the street. I looked back at the frightening lady.

When Dad came home from work that night, we told him the latest story about Blackie and how we were afraid of the neighbor lady and feared she would hurt our crow.

"She said, 'black and evil?'" Dad asked.

"Uh-huh," we agreed.

"Well, from now on, take your normal route to school, but when you get close to her house, cross the street. Blackie will follow you. After you pass her house, take your normal route. I don't want you ever walking in front of her house on the same side of the road again. Do you understand me?"

"Yeah, we understand, but why did she keep yelling 'black and evil,' and why was Blackie enjoying his ant bath?"

"Answering the ant bath question is easy. Answering your question about her attitude is complicated. Some birds know that certain ants help them. These ants give off a liquid when their nest is being invaded. It so happens that this liquid helps the birds. It kills off tiny insects and germs that are on the bird. It soothes the bird's skin. That's why Blackie was taking an ant bath."

"Now, as far as what the lady said, some folks simply do not like black things," our father explained. "You've probably heard that black cats bring bad luck? Did you know that black dogs are the last ones in a pound to be adopted? Black bats are shown to be scary at Halloween. Everyone fears Black Widow Spiders. Why even black licorice isn't popular. Sadly, some folks are even afraid of black people. There's no reason for it. They just are. I think that lady up the road is one of them. She doesn't like anything black, and well, Blackie is black. Do you understand? I want you and that bird staying away from her."

And so, we did.

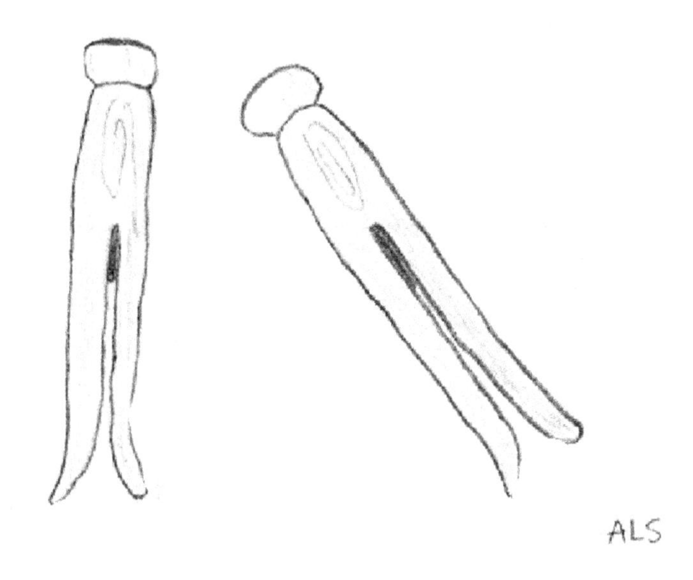

Chapter 5

First Flights

As Blackie's wing healed, we observed him advance from walking and hopping to loping with some wing flaps. Blackie soon learned his wing flaps got him some elevation. He learned that flight provided him with new opportunities for mischief.[18] His first flights took him to the top of the ladder of his cage. He no longer needed to walk up his ladder to get into his cage. He flew to it.

Soon when we went to our backyard and called him,

instead of walking towards us, he zoomed towards us in flight. If we did not put out an outstretched arm as a perch, Blackie would just land on our heads. Walt and I learned to put out an arm as we called him. His claws never hurt us, but they were quite strong. It was joyful to have a bird land on our arms. It always made us smile.

Back in those days, folks did not have clothes dryers. Instead, they had tall, metal poles planted and spread out in their back yards. At the top of these poles, rope was attached leading from one pole to another. It was called a clothesline. Our poles were set up in the shape of a diamond in our backyard. Our clothesline poles also served as bases when we played kickball and baseball out back.

After a load of clothes was washed, the clean laundry was carried outside in a basket. In another small basket were clothespins. They were not really pins. They looked more like small wooden clamps. People would take out an item of damp laundry, give it a flip shake, and then attach it to the clothesline with the clothespins.

Depending on the weather, sometimes the clothes were wind and sun dried and ready to be taken down within an hour. Sometimes it would take a little longer. If a storm popped up, it was considered a family emergency, and everyone would run outside trying to get the laundry off the lines before it all got drenched by the storm.

My favorite part of drying clothes on a clothesline was the smell. Line-dried laundry smells different. It smells pure. As I would help take down the dry clothes, I'd smell every single item I removed. To this day, I can close my eyes and remember exactly how it smelled. I miss that aroma.

Blackie also loved the clothesline. Once he was able to fly to its height, he considered it one gigantic perch. As we would hang up or take down clothes, Blackie would perch on a section of the rope and caw and caw. He sounded happy.

It seemed as if Blackie's voice was changing. When he was a youngster, his caw seemed higher, nasally, and funny sounding. Now his caws sounded like other crows. He would joyfully caw and sidestep along the clothesline and watch us.

We realized Blackie was not just watching us doing our chore, he was observing and learning. Blackie constantly watched and learned. Curiosity is a valuable trait even for birds. When a creature is curious, it can learn a lesson.

He watched us hang up and take down clothes using the

clothespins. It did not take him long to figure out that he could help us by removing the clothespins. Yep, there were many times we went outside to bring in the line-dried clothes to find the sheets, towels, and all the clothing lying all over the grass. Neatly below the clothesline we found the clothespins.

Walt and I would sometimes be able to spy on Blackie and catch him in the act. He would approach a clothespin with caution, grab it, and faster than we could yell, he would lift the pin and drop it to the ground and then sidestep to remove the next one. When the laundry item he liberated[19] landed on the ground, Blackie would stare at it from his clothesline perch and let out three loud caws. He seemed so proud.

Often, even when clothes were not hanging on the line, Blackie flew to the rope and perched. Frequently he did the strangest thing. He spread out both wings and faced the sun. He looked completely relaxed, almost napping. Then he would turn around and sun his other side. It was as if he knew how to position himself for maximum sun exposure. He looked calm and comfortable. Every now and then, he prodded under his wings. He picked and poked from chest to tail. Reaching the tip of his tail was difficult, but when he reached it, he slid every tail feather between his beak. If he nudged off an errant[20] bug, he promptly ate it.

When Blackie held this position, he reminded me of American Indian totems.[21] Up north, where our family cabin was located, the land had been settled by the Shawnee tribe of American Indians. I loved going to that cabin and search for pottery shards and arrow heads. I never found any, but I kept on looking.

One of my favorite places to go when we were there was a local store that carried art of the Shawnee. There were many miniature totems to purchase. Every totem was hand carved. Some were painted. Some were not. Many had ravens and crows with outstretched wings and prominent beaks as part of their design. Those totems always caught my eye because they reminded me of Blackie sitting on the clothesline taking in the sun.

Years later, I learned that ravens and crows are revered by American Indians. The birds were known to be wise and smart. I think the American Indians were wise and smart too for figuring that out and including the birds in their artwork.

Chapter 6

Higher Flights Lead to Greater Mischief

In a few months, Blackie was able to fly as well as the wild neighborhood crows and joined them occasionally. Walking and hopping were no longer required. He spent equal time with his crow friends as he did with his human friends. He went wherever he wanted to go. The bulk of his days were spent doing crow things and being naughty. At night, he roosted in his safe cage in our elm tree.

Now Blackie could sense fear in other beings, and he

delighted in striking it into other creatures. It did not matter what kind of creature or its size. He was not mean. He just found joy in terrorizing others. I swear that bird had a dark sense of humor.[22]

One such creature was my friend Maddie. She lived several doors up from me, and we loved playing together. Outside or inside, it did not matter. Sometimes she had dinner with us, but most of the time she walked home when dinnertime came. One day she left at her usual time to walk home. About a half-hour after she left, her Mom called asking if Maddie was still at our house.

"No." my Mom said. "She left here about thirty minutes ago. I'll send Amy out to look for her. She probably stopped off at someone else's house." Mom could sense the fear in Maddie's mother.

As I slipped on my jacket, I could hear Blackie hollering up a storm. One. Two. Three caws. Again, and again. "Caw! Caw! Caw!" I looked out our side window. There was Maddie with her arms held out at shoulder height with our crow perched on top of her head. "Caw! Caw! Caw!" Maddie had a look of terror on her face and tears ran down her cheeks. She was too afraid to move. Poor Maddie. She was always a little bit timid. Blackie sensed it, and that night he chose to tease her. I ran outside and held my arm up for Blackie to perch. He did so immediately, grabbing a small amount of Maddie's curly blond hair while doing so. Thank goodness Maddie was free. She ran in the direction of her house wiping away tears from her face and rubbing her head. To this day, I have no idea what her parents' reaction was when they heard her story, but it seemed like I was invited to play more often at her house than she did at mine.

Blackie also took joy in untying shoes. Actually, not just untying shoes. If allowed, he unlaced them. He often flew over to our feet as we sat in the grass. First, he checked to see if we had any treats for him to eat. If not, he headed straight to our shoes. He untied the bow faster than we could shoo him away. Then he started on the knot. Untying it was not difficult for him. The challenge he faced was pulling the shoestring out of the grommets.[23] If we tied our shoes especially tight, he pecked and pecked at the shoestring. By doing so, the grommet slowly released its tight grip on the shoelace. He worked and worked at it until the victory of a free shoelace was his. Walt and I learned that perseverance was often rewarded.

That bird taught me a lot about patience way before I

even knew the meaning of the word. He did not give up or fly away in frustration. He worked on that shoelace until he got it. Never giving up on achieving a goal seemed like an important lesson of life.

The mischievous game that nearly caused our Dad to get rid of our crow was Blackie's fascination with windshield wipers. Not the metal part that swoops. It was the attached rubber part that fascinated him. To Blackie, it must have looked like a snake. I cannot tell you how many windshield wiper blades Blackie ripped off cars. It seemed like a weekly occurrence. We would get a call from a neighbor.

Mom usually answered the phone and after a minute she would say, "Hon, it's for you. Blackie did it again."

Dad would take the phone and ask in a gruff manner, "Yeah?"

Walt and I then heard loud, muffled noises coming from the phone. Our Dad took a softer tone and told the person to let him know how much it cost. Either Walt or I would then be sent to the person's house with cash in an envelope. This went on and on. Blackie killed the vicious serpent, and we reimbursed its owner.

We were not a poor family, but we were not wealthy.

We "lived within our budget"[24] whatever that meant. Money going out weekly for the damage our crow did became burdensome.[25]

One day, after receiving one of those phone calls, my Dad ordered my brother "go get a hold of that darn crow and bring him into the car." Walt did as he was told, and they pulled out of the driveway. They were gone quite a while. When they returned, Walt still held Blackie and released him as soon as he opened the car door. I was confused. My Mom went and talked to my Dad while I went and talked to my brother.

"What happened Walt? Where did you go?"

"Amy, Dad was mad. That was like the tenth time Blackie ripped off a windshield wiper blade. We drove up to Rosslyn Farms. Do you know where that is?"

"Uh, huh. That's pretty far away on the way to Uncle Bill's house. Right?" I asked.

"Yeah, Dad said we were going to release Blackie there. Dad said he was tired of all the money the bird was costing us with his naughty habit of ripping off the blades."

Fear set into me. "Get rid of Blackie? But, Daddy always said Blackie would leave us when Blackie knew it was time." My eyes filled with tears.

“Don’t worry Amy. Dad changed his mind when I asked him when the hunting season is for crows.” Walt said with a sly grin. “As soon as I asked Dad that question, he turned the car around, and we came back here. It’s all good.”

I was relieved. Blackie got a pass. The funny thing about Blackie being nearly let go, I swear he learned a lesson. I often wondered if that bird could read my Dad’s mind. Did he sense what my Dad had planned for him? He never again ripped off another wiper blade. Sure, he would still land on cars, but he kept his misbehaving to cawing loudly and leaving a white deposit on top of the car. When people called and complained to Mom and Dad about his new type of mischief, it cost my parents nothing. Walt or I would be sent to clean up the gift he left on their cars.

Chapter 7

"Mary had a Little Lamb," but…

Blackie no longer walked us to school. As Walt and I headed up Foxcroft Hill on our way to school, Blackie flew from tree to tree leading the way, always staying a little bit ahead of us. I am not sure if he was showing off or just making sure we did not get lost.

Blackie became the students' superstar. Everyone wanted to see him…everyone except certain teachers. I was lucky. My teacher, Mrs. Pettit, loved Blackie. Everyone should have a first-grade teacher like Mrs. Pettit. She was large and loud and happy. She found joy in everything and every child. I remember her teaching about the launch of *Sputnik.*[26] I do not remember her detailed lesson. Only the highlights. "Russia…spaceship...science is important…one day…Moon…USA." She made quite an impression.

As I was saying, Mrs. Pettit loved Blackie. She encouraged students to save a scrap of their lunch or an old pencil nub to give to Blackie. Whosever turn it was set out their gift on the classroom's window ledge. Sure enough, Blackie soon came and snatched it up. It became a daily occurrence. Our class observed him, and then drew our attention back to Mrs. Pettit. Yep, every child should have a teacher like Mrs. Pettit. She did not compete with him for our attention. She included him.

Now Blackie learned quickly. Soon he flew to every classroom's window ledge looking for gifts. Some students who had teachers who did not appreciate Blackie would sneak food onto the ledge.

Blackie's appearance created mayhem[27] in those classrooms. The teachers would run about shouting ridiculous orders. Much like the "Wizard of Oz," they yelled statements such as, "Don't pay attention to the crow. Look at me." Those teachers would run to the side of the classroom lowering the shades and raising their voices, anything to hold their class's attention. They should have done what Mrs. Pettit did. Welcome and include Blackie.

One day Walt and I were summoned together to the principal's office. Miss Smith told us to be seated and began asking us about Blackie. Our feet didn't touch the floor as we sat in the chairs. Walt was nine. I was six. Miss Smith was a gazillion years old. We were terrified. Walt and I had never been in trouble before, and here we were both in trouble at the same time. We did not stand a chance.

"Is he your pet?" Miss Smith asked.

Walt and I proudly stated, "Yes."

"Do you bring him to school?" She wanted to know.

"No, he flies here by himself," we said to our principal.

"Are you aware of the chaos[28] he causes?" she asked.

Walt and I shrugged. "What's chaos?"

"Do you feed him?"

That seemed like a silly question for her to ask.

"At home, we give him some food, and he finds some on his own," Walt said with pride.

"Are you going to keep him?" Miss Smith asked, her

voice rising.

"Our Dad says Blackie will decide when it's time to leave," we explained to our principal.

Miss Smith had a stern look on her face as she said, "Teachers have been complaining about him. From now on, I do not want your pet to come to Foxcroft. Do you understand me?"

Walt and I looked at each other. Yes, we understood her, but neither of us had any idea how to control his actions, so we did what kids normally do in situations like this. We shrugged our shoulders and gave out a non-committal, "UNuh-huh."

Word must have gotten out about us getting in trouble. We were celebrities among our peers. We had street cred. We survived a trip to the principal's office.

Mrs. Pettit heard too, and she was none too pleased when she heard two little kids got in trouble for something they could not control. Her next move was genius. Mrs. Pettit called the local newspaper, *The Signal Item*, and invited a reporter to our classroom. Shortly after she called, a photographer, Vic Polk, showed up to our class. Mrs. Pettit's eyes had a devilish look about them. Mr. Polk introduced himself to our class and summarized his job.

Then he asked our class if we knew about a famous crow.

The class roared, "Blackie!"

Mrs. Pettit handed me a note and told me to give it to my brother's teacher. Now Walt had a teacher who did not appreciate our pet. After reading the note, Walt's teacher dismissed him and said he was to go with me and report to Mrs. Pettit. When Walt and I returned, the photographer asked my brother if he could get Blackie.

Walt said, "I could try. He's usually here at this time because it's close to lunchtime."

Mrs. Pettit smiled knowingly.

Walt and I went outside, and he called Blackie. In less than a minute, our crow flew around from the back of the building and landed on Walt's out-stretched arm.

Dad taught us how to safely hold a crow so you have control of him without hurting the bird. I watched as Walt did this. As Blackie perched, Walt slowly and gently circled his fingers around Blackie's legs. He moved the bird close to his chest so Blackie could not flap his wings, and we petted him and said soothing things to him. The photographer came out and took photographs of the three of us. Blackie did not struggle or squawk. It looked to me like Blackie enjoyed the attention and posed for the camera.

The photographer encouraged us to bring Blackie into the classroom. Walt and I hesitated. Blackie had never been inside a building. Never. But being obedient kids, we did as we were told, and Walt marched inside holding onto Blackie while I followed him. At first Blackie was calm and curious. Then one kid, who I never liked, let out an ear-piercing shriek which startled our crow. Blackie got away from my brother's grasp and flew in circles around the classroom looking for an escape route. Some of his swoops were high. Some were low and barely above the students' heads. I remember he flew above the heads of Patti, Marcia, Skippy, and Dougie. They were elated. They smiled, clapped their hands, and squealed with delight. One classmate, Luisa, who later went on to become a kindergarten teacher at Foxcroft, went to comfort those students who were frightened. Another girl, Judy, ducked for cover under her desk. Her wise move to escape Blackie must have impressed my brother, because fifteen years later my brother married that girl. Around and around Blackie flew. He spotted what he thought was freedom and flew straight into the window. He did this again and again. Walt and I were panicked, terrified, and afraid our crow would hurt himself. We knew birds have been known to fly into windows and die from the damage they inflict on themselves when they impacted. The photographer was smiling. He did not realize Blackie's danger. Mrs. Pettit had a look of concern on her face. She shared Walt's and my distress.

After, what seemed like hours, but was only minutes, Blackie throttled full speed, one final time, into the window. This time, he collapsed onto the floor. After this final collision with the window, Walt rushed over and swept up Blackie in his arms. I held the door that led to the outside for Walt and Blackie. The three of us rushed out of the classroom to the safe outdoors. Walt held Blackie close until our bird's breathing slowed down, and then Walt released our crow. Blackie flew to the nearest, tall telephone pole. He shuffled his feathers several times as if to get rid of all the fear and indignity he felt. He stayed a while, and then flew back in the direction of our house.

Mrs. Pettit joined us. "Is Blackie going to be okay?"

"Yes," we said in unison.

"He just got a little scared," I said.

"Good," she said, and we all went back into the school.

A week or so later, Walt and I were on page six of *The Signal Item*. There was a picture of Walt, Blackie, and me.

Under the photograph, the headline read, "Everywhere that Amy and Walter go… Mary had a little lamb, but Amy and Walter Leput have a crow that goes to school with them at Foxcroft." Then, as I remember, there was some nonsense written about how our principal welcomed the bird.

Blackie, Walt, and I were famous. We made our school famous. Our principal was happy with the attention our crow earned for her school. It was our fifteen minutes of fame.

Yep, every child should have a first-grade teacher like Mrs. Pettit. She set things right.

Chapter 8

Gifts and Affection

Another lesson Blackie taught me was how a person does not always get what they want. You see, I was envious that Blackie talked to my Dad. Well, not really talked, but mimicked him. Sure, when Walt or I would run into Blackie's territory he would greet us with a variety of caws. Usually, it was a pair of caws. "Caw! Caw!" Sometimes it was three or four. When he was upset that there was an intruder in our yard, he would let loose with several caws strung together. "Caw! Caw! Caw! Caw!" His crow vocabulary was not just limited to caws. At times, he would make funny rattling noises, other times it sounded like he was growling. Occasionally he made cooing sounds. The sound I wanted most to hear from Blackie was the sound he used to greet my father. I never received it.

Dad returned home from work every day at 4 o'clock. That crow magically appeared at that time and landed on top of our garage. The moment Dad opened the car door, Blackie addressed my Dad with a human-sounding, "Hel'lo!" *Every Day*.

In response, my father said it back to him, "Hel'lo!" As my Dad walked into the house, he shook his head in disbelief, with a smile on his face. Their exchange continued until Dad left Blackie's sight.

Then I tried. I said it exactly as they did which is not the way most people greet each other. Blackie and my father's greeting was louder on the first part of the word. In later years of schooling, I learned this was called an "accented syllable." Over and over again I would try to get that bird to mimic me. He never did. Not one time. When I was young, I did not know what a good lesson it was that you do not always get what you want. "Boy, that bird is stubborn,"[29] I thought to myself. I only knew the meaning of that word because my mother often said that about me. It seems that being stubborn is good if you are the one doing it, but it is not good when you are the one receiving it. I believe that to this day.

They say animals form special bonds with one particular person. In our house, it was my Dad. Do not get me wrong. Blackie liked Walt, Mom, and me. After all, we fed and entertained him, but his soul was connected to my Dad's. It was my father who was the recipient of not just "Hellos," but also of gifts. I was glad I was not the recipient of some of his presents. Blackie's gift preference was rodents. Not mice. Rats!

My brother first witnessed Blackie's gift-giving. Walt and my father were in the garage moving around scrap wood. Blackie was perched on a shovel that hung on the wall. It was hot and Blackie's beak was wide open. Some birds do that when they are hot. They do not sweat or pant. They keep their beaks open in order to get cool. All of a sudden, Walt moved a piece of wood and out scurried a baby rat. As the rat tried to make his escape through the open garage door, my Dad shouted an order to Blackie, "Get him!" Understanding my Dad's order, Blackie swooped down from his perch and landed on the baby rat. In one snip, the rat was beheaded.[30] Blackie stared at the two parts as if he were evaluating them. He chose the rat's head, picked it up with his beak, hopped over to my Father, and dropped it at his feet. Blackie had a look of loyalty as he stared at Dad when he dropped the head near him.

"Then," Walt said, "Blackie returned to the remainder of the rat's body, got a good grip on it and flew away. He did not get very high carrying all that weight, and he sure was gone for a long time."

As Walt retold what he had observed, I was so filled with wonderment and mental images, all I could say was, "Wow!"

I got to witness the second rat offering. My father and I were in the basement. Dad was puttering around in his workshop tinkering on a project. I was nearby tinkering on my own. The weather was nice outside, so the heavy door was open with only the screen door shut. All of a sudden we heard, "Whoop. Whoop. Whoop." Yes, you can hear wind get pushed by a crow's wings. "Whoop. Whoop. Whoop."

Then Blackie started his cawing in earnest. "Caw! Caw! Caw!...Caw! Caw! Caw!" over and over again.

My Dad came out of his workshop and said to me, "Come on. Let's go see what Blackie is into this time."

The screen door screeched as we pushed it open. There

on the floor of the walk-up stairs was a dead rat. Not a baby rat. It was a full-grown rat. Fortunately, Blackie made sure it was not moving before he dropped his offering. Then Blackie started with his boastful cawing again.

He continued on and on until my Dad said, "All right, all right. Thank you."

Upon hearing Dad's gratitude, Blackie flew away with what, I swear, looked like a "You're welcome" expression on his face.

Dad ordered me to go get the shovel out of the garage. As I ran to do it, I heard Dad cussing and muttering about the nearby local farm that was being torn down.

When a farm, and all its outbuildings[31] are leveled, the rodents who resided there are misplaced. They scurry about looking for new housing. Unlike those of us who lived near the old farm, Blackie was appreciative of the rats scampering to find a new home. It was a plentiful food source for him.

Years later, where that old farm used to be, a high school was built. Both Walt and I attended that high school. Every time I entered through one of the school's back doors, I wondered which farm building had been there and how many rats passed through that same threshold.[32]

Chapter 9

The Unknown Known

You need to understand something about our Dad. He had a touch of St. Francis of Assisi about him. In the Catholic church, St. Francis of Assisi is the patron saint of animals. That was our Dad. He was drawn to animals, and they were drawn to him. Between them existed instinctive,[33] trust and understanding.

What brought a smile to our Dad's face, along with him ordering us to, "Come on. Hurry up. You have to see this," was witnessing an act of Mother Nature.[34] He delighted in watching animals' behaviors and interactions. If we were called to observe, Walt and I would stand next to Dad and watch the animal that held our father's attention. We knew to move slowly and quietly so as not to disturb the animals. Dad would whisper in our ears and explain what we were gifted in seeing. At times it was wild male turkeys vying for the attention of some hens. They look like they are the size of black bears when they do that. Other times we saw rabbits perform a three-foot vertical jump as part of their courtship, and then later we were permitted to watch a live birth of the new bunnies. Countless times we saw birds eat seed out of our father's hand.

Every so often the act of Mother Nature was not kind. We saw our share of predator versus prey.[35] Dad would warn us what we were going to witness, and then we could decide whether or not we wanted to see it. I do not remember Walt or me ever refusing to witness an act of Mother Nature, be it kind or not.

Dad would explain how rough it is for wild animals. We would hear phrases like, "'Hunt and be hunted.' 'Maternal instinct.'[36] 'All animals must eat.' 'Only the strongest survive.' 'Mange.'[37] 'The Circle of Life.'[38] 'Predator versus Prey.'" We would not just hear those phrases. We understood and accepted them. Dad would provide a brief, hushed explanation as we watched the lesson unfold. He and Mother Nature were great teachers of life and death.

From the day Blackie came into our lives, we knew there would be a day when he would depart. No one dwelled on it. Dad would just periodically remind us that Blackie would decide when it was time to leave and become a full-time wild crow. It was a valuable lesson that Blackie was on loan. We knew Blackie would one day prefer to be among other wild crows more than he wanted to be among us. With this lesson, Blackie's eventual departure was not frightening; rather, it was normal and expected. If anyone asked about our plans for our crow, Walt and I simply shrugged and said, "Blackie will decide." They were not just words we echoed. It was a truth and acceptance that came from our core.[39]

One day Walt was playing with some of his buddies about halfway up the hill to our school. It was during spring when trees start their budding. He heard a familiar, "Caw! Caw! Caw!" Walt watched as Blackie flew with some other crows chasing away a hawk. This was a common sight. Blackie often hung out with other crow groupings. Walt did not think much about it other than he noticed that Blackie was flying in the direction of Glendale, the area of town where our father was raised.

It was a few days later that our family realized that Blackie was not coming around to our home. Dad announced it was breeding season for crows and more than likely Blackie had spotted his mate for life. It was not a sad realization or proclamation.[40] It was a matter of fact. We were not sad. We all were accepting of Blackie's choice. It was time for him to move and change. We knew the unknown course he decided to take. It was the way of nature.

Dad decided to leave the cage set up in the tree in case Blackie would return or if it was ever needed for another reason. Seeing the empty cage over the years was not sad. It bore witness to a wonderful time of our lives when we were privileged to share in a crow's life. I only hoped that Blackie would somehow be able to tell his babies about our family, our shared experiences, our care and love of him, and that we could be trusted.

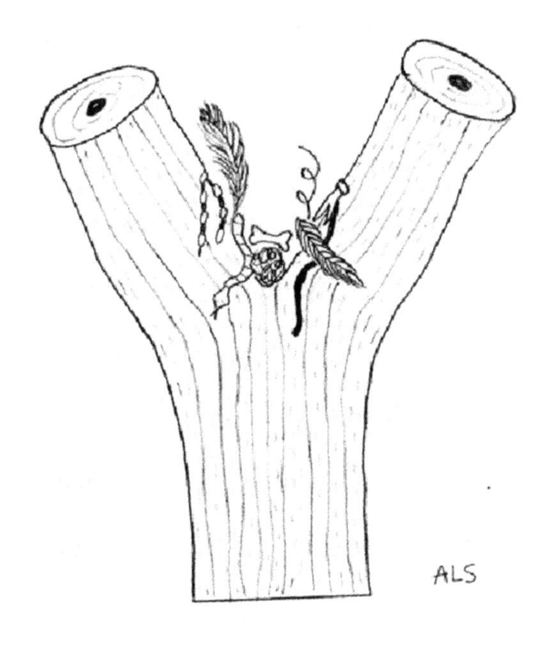

Chapter 10

Treasures and Gifts

That old cage of Blackie's stayed in place for years. Every now and then, an adventurous, stray critter would go inside. They would not stay long. It was almost as if they knew it was the former home of a revered[41] creature. They would hop from perch to perch, side to side and eventually make their way out.

Ten years that cage stayed in place. Walt went off to college. I became a teenager. Whenever we looked at the cage, nostalgia[42] filled our hearts and smiles appeared on our faces. We caught ourselves saying to each other, "Remember when Blackie…?" and we would smile.

As the elm tree grew taller and taller, the cage aged in place, and it almost became part of the crook in the tree. One night a fierce windstorm came through our neighborhood. The next day unfamiliar debris was scattered all over our yard. Mom, Dad, and I picked up the rubble that had fallen in our yard and our neighbors' yards. Uncle John towed it away. One task remained. Our beloved elm tree, the one holding Blackie's cage, was uprooted. I looked at Dad and asked, "What are we going to do with the tree?"

"We will wait until your brother comes home, and we'll haul it out of here piece by piece. For now, stay away from it. It might be dangerous."

I must have given him an eyeroll, because then my Dad clearly stated, "I am not kidding Amy. I know how much you still love to climb trees, but that tree is unstable and broken. You stay away from it. I'll let you help Walt and me with its removal."

A month or so passed and Walt returned home from college. A few days later, we set out to safely remove the dead tree. We started off with what used to be the top of the tree. Walt or Dad used the chainsaw and cut off manageable-sized pieces. One by one, we dragged the pieces onto the trailer. It took several days. Finally, we got to the crook in the tree where the cage still clung. Walt and Dad worked together removing nails and screws. Tugging and pausing, banging and unscrewing, finally and ironically, they used a crowbar to free the aviary. The old elm tree finally loosened its grip on the cage, and out came Blackie's home. We walked over to the tree's elbow that had housed the cage. Simultaneously, we all spotted a stash of treasures nestled in the crook of that tree.

"Well, I'll be," Dad exclaimed. "Look what that crazy crow left us." We had heard crows kept treasures, but, until that moment, we never found Blackie's cache.[43] We started to remove his treasures one by one. Out came a dry-rotted windshield wiper blade, a clothespin, a small chain, a snake's shed skin, a ball of aluminum foil, several crow feathers, a shoelace, a dehydrated rat tail, a rodent skull, a praying mantis egg case, a chicken bone, a pencil stub, and I swear, a curly blonde hair from Maddie's head. Every one was a gem. A treasure. A gift from our crow. The ten years since his departure melted away, and we all were crying and laughing at the same time. He was the pet of a lifetime.

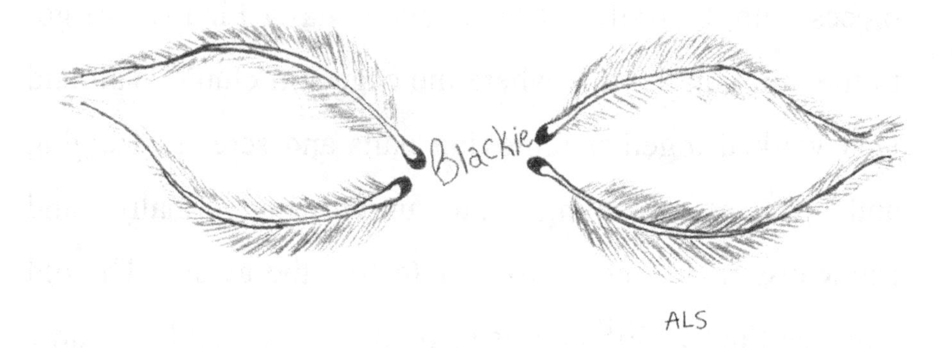

Epilogue

Forever

Walt and I became adults, got married, and had children. From time to time, our spouses and sons heard Blackie tales. They learned of the joys, wonderments, and lessons that crow added to our lives.

On one Summer Solstice, Walt called me up with the news that our Dad had passed away.[44] It was not a surprise. He had been ill for a few months. Still, it was way too soon. I remember kneeling on the floor with my head buried into the bed and crying from a source within my body that I did not know existed. Only those who have lost a deeply attached loved one know that sound. It is primal. It cannot be duplicated. I only uttered it once again when our Mom was dying.

I was alone that afternoon when I learned of my Dad's death. My husband and sons were practicing baseball at a local ballfield. I had the wherewithal to walk to a neighbor's and ask for a ride to the ballfield. I knew not to risk driving, but I needed my husband's arms around me. As I got out of the car and walked towards my husband, he looked at me, and he knew. His arms surrounded me as I whispered, "He's gone." We quietly stayed in place for several minutes.

Softly, from a distance I heard cawing. I broke away from my husband and looked up. A family of four crows flew above us, over the field, and onward to the direction of a local chapel. "Come on." I said. "They're leading the way. Dad is with them."

Our family walked to the chapel, and we sat on a pew thinking about a great man. I was stunned and silent, yet oddly, those neighborhood crows provided me with a little bit of joy that day alongside the grief. The wish I made as a child, hoping that Blackie would teach his offspring about the joy-filled adventures with our family, came true. Our crow had passed on his experiences about our care and love for him. He taught his offspring that we could be trusted. Those crows who guided us to the chapel that day were taking care of us just as they had been taught. Blackie had passed on to his babies, and they told their babies, and so on, "Those two humans, Walt and Amy, they can be trusted."

It was no surprise to me when later I read about a wildlife scientist's study about crows. John Marzluff proved that crows do pass on to each other, and to their offspring, information about people who can be trusted and those who cannot. I was delighted to read the results of his experiments, but honestly, I believed this for a long time.

Over sixty years have passed since we shared our lives with Blackie. To this day, when I go outside, crows greet me. Every time and all the time when I go for a walk, I hear a crow's acknowledgment. I believe they are telling each other, "That woman. That man. They are safe. They are crow friends. They will never harm you."

And, they are correct.

"The Bird that had Gumption!"

Blackie was the bravest of birds,
because he could not fly.
A dog who did not care for him
decided that he should die.

But Blackie had the will to live
and fought his handicap.
He became the neighborhood pet
which was a big mishap.

Through the months that he healed his wing
he lived in my backyard.
He was known to be mischievous
and took wipers off the cars.

He loved to follow me to school
and land on my friends' heads.
Because he knew when he would sing
that he would get some bread.

Blackie was the slyest of crows;
he loved to untie shoes.
Clothespins were his favorite sport
to take them when we snoozed.

The mating call rang in his ears
which gave him the strength to fly.
Away he flew in early March,
and we said our last good-bye.

—written by Amy –age 7 and her cousin, Nancy Grejda

Bibliography

Marzluff, John, et al. "Lasting Recognition of Threatening People by Wild American Crows."
Animal Behaviour, pp. 699-707, 2009

Polk, Vic. "Everywhere That Amy and Walter Go…" *The Signal Item,* December 19, 1957, page 6

Westerfield, Michael. *The Language of Crows*. Willimantic, CT: Ashford Press, 2017. Print.

Acknowledgements

My brother, Walt Leput, had several memories of Blackie that I did not remember. Thanks Walt.

My father, Pete Leput, instilled love, appreciation, and curiosity of nature. It has been a gift that has lasted a lifetime.

My mother, Emily Krok Leput, provided weekly trips to the Bookmobile or The Andrew Carnegie Free Library & Music Hall in Carnegie, PA. She encouraged and satisfied my love of learning and reading, and she definitely taught me how to use an Encyclopedia.

Ben and Brian, my sons—You two continue to make me want to be a better person.

Patti Hall Carothers, from my first-grade class, who encouraged me to write this memoir. Blackie's flight in our first-grade classroom was memorable to her too.

Rita of Rita Hogan Photography, Copperas Cove, TX for bringing the old photos back to life so they could be used in this book.

My writing muse, Janet Maldonado, thank you for your tactful suggestions.

JoLynne Dougherty, of the Andrew Carnegie Free Library and Music Hall in Carnegie, PA who voluntarily researched the local newspaper archives.

Shawn Bergman, of "Canuck and I" Facebook fame, whose chronicle of the strong relationship between man and crow touched people worldwide.

Author Biography

Amy Leput Strahl's youth was spent in the suburbs of Pittsburgh, PA where her life with Blackie occurred.

She has two degrees in education and spent decades teaching. Although she is now retired, she freely imbues bits of knowledge to willing and unwilling recipients.

She and her husband, of nearly five decades, Robert, reside in Maryland.

For Teachers

For those teachers who would like to use this book in class, you can email the author to acquire a teacher's guide.

It includes chapter summaries, detailed lesson plans, required visual aids, and other resource suggestions.

blackiethecrow18@gmail.com

EVERYWHERE THAT AMY AND WALTER GO . . . Mary had a little lamb, but Amy and Walter Leput have a crow that go to school with them at Foxcroft. It has become accustomed to the classroom, likes to break pencils, and consume the lunchbox leftovers. They have named it Blackie.

Signal-Item Photo by Vic Folk

Endnotes Glossary

[1] **ornery:** minor troublemaker

[2] **put down:** painlessly induce death in order to eliminate pain and misery

[3] **roadkill:** the dead body of an animal found on the side of a road usually struck
accidentally by a motor vehicle

[4] **adjective:** a word that describes a person, place or thing

[5] **gape:** inside the mouth where the two jawbones meet

[6] **scoff:** made fun of

[7] **forage:** look for food

[8] **confined:** restricted in movement

[9] **stability:** strength and support

[10] **utterances:** quiet remarks

[11] **uncanny:** mysterious

[12] **grating:** annoying

[13] **body language**: bodily positions that communicate feelings without the use of words

[14] **noggin:** slang term meaning one's head

[15] **gauge** : estimate

[16] **irresistible:** tempting

[17] **menacing:** frightening and mean

[18] **mischief:** playful misbehaving

[19] **liberated:** freed

[20] **errant:** stray

[21] **totems:** an object that represents a group or clan

[22] **dark sense of humor:** a type of humor that is mildly offensive yet is still funny

[23] **grommets:** rings or eyelets through which shoelaces pass

[24] **lived within our budget:** not spend more money than earned

[25] **burdensome:** difficult

[26] **Sputnik:** the first manmade satellite. It was launched by Russia in 1957.

[27] **mayhem:** trouble

[28] **chaos**: disorder and confusion

[29] **stubborn:** bullheaded and rebellious

[30] **beheaded:** one's head is cut off

[31] **outbuildings:** buildings found on a farm that have a particular purpose

[32] **threshold:** entrance way into a building

[33] **instinctive:** a natural awareness of something without being taught

[34] **Mother Nature:** the world around us that is not man made

[35] **predator versus prey:** when an animal hunts, stalks, kills, and eats another animal

[36] **maternal instinct:** the protective feeling a mother has of her offspring

[37] **mange:** a skin infection that causes an animal's fur loss which can cause the animal to get deadly infections

[38] **Circle of Life:** when something dies, its death can help another

[39] **came from our cores:** deep down, absolute truth and belief

[40] **proclamation:** a declared statement

[41] **revered:** respected

[42] **nostalgia:** to remember the happiness of a former place or time

[43] **cache**: a hiding place used for storage

[44] **passed away:** died

CPSIA information can be obtained
at www.ICGtesting.com
Printed in the USA
BVHW040546171121
621781BV00012B/838

9 781633 635296